Broken Chains

by
Quincy Howe

GLOBE FEARON
EDUCATIONAL PUBLISHER
PARAMUS, NEW JERSEY

Paramount Publishing

Cover Illustrators: Keaf Holliday/Fred Willingham
Supervising Editor: Steve Feinstein
Project Editor: Renee Beach
Production Manager: Penny Gibson
Manufacturing Supervisor: Della Smith
Senior Production Editor: Linda Greenberg
Production Editor: Alan Dalgleish
Interior Design and Production: Margarita Giammanco
Art Direction: Nancy Sharkey
Marketing: Marge Curson

Printed in the United States of America
2 3 4 5 6 7 8 9 10   99 98 97 96 95

ISBN 0-835-91088-1

GLOBE FEARON
EDUCATIONAL PUBLISHER
PARAMUS, NEW JERSEY

Paramount Publishing

Table of Contents

A Breakfast Date

Julio and I were sitting in a small neighborhood diner. Julio had never really had a girlfriend. This had always bothered him. He's a really sweet guy. The girls always like him because he is kind and gentle. He talks a macho line. Yet, even he does not believe it.

Anyway, at the same time I had met Charmian, Julio met her friend Vanessa. Charmian and I became a real item. We liked each other right away. Julio and Vanessa had eyes for each other, too. But they had been slow about getting together. Neither one wanted to get hurt. Both Charmian and I thought that Vanessa and Julio would make a good couple. We wanted to do everything we could to move things along. This morning, for example, Charmian was bringing Vanessa with her. The four of us were going to have breakfast together. Julio was both excited and angry.

"Man, Vesey," he said, "you don't have to go out and find a woman for me. I can hook up my own girls without you bringing Vanessa all the way to the Bronx from Manhattan."

"You're right, Julio," I said. "I can call Charmian right now and tell her to forget about bringing Vanessa. The call will get through in time. Anyway, Vanessa is sort of a dog. I don't think she's right for you."

Now I really had him! "Nobody talks about Vanessa that way. She is beautiful!" When he realized what he was saying, he became embarrassed. He paused for a moment and then went on. "OK, OK, so I like her. But that doesn't mean that I need to have you setting up meetings for me. I can just call her on the phone when I want to see her."

"Yeah," I said, "I noticed how many times you have called her. Just once. And, you've only gone out with her once."

Julio knew I was right. I could see he felt that I was taking advantage of him. "It's all right, man," I said. "You will never admit this, even in your sleep, but you can be shy sometimes. Believe me, a girl likes that."

He just sat there, quietly. He knew there was no place for this discussion to go. After about 15 minutes, I saw Charmian and Vanessa coming down the sidewalk toward the diner. They came in the door. They joined us at the table. Charmian gave me a little kiss and said hello to Julio. I said hello to Charmian and Vanessa. Julio and Vanessa said nothing to one another. They were too embarrassed.

Actually, I was surprised at Vanessa. Normally, you couldn't shut her up. Finally, she looked over at Julio and said, "So, Julio, whazzup?"

He looked uncomfortable. After a long silence he said, "Not much. Just chillin'."

I looked over at Charmian. I could see she was having a hard time to keep from laughing. We had agreed to say nothing so that Julio and Vanessa would have to talk.

We ordered our food. Everyone sat quietly until it came. Finally, after a few more minutes, Vanessa said to Julio, "Could you pass the salt, please?"

Julio was so nervous that when he did it, he knocked over her glass. Half of her orange juice went down into her lap. Julio grabbed the napkin holder. He ripped out about 20 napkins. Then he jumped out of his seat. He was all set to wipe up the spill.

Suddenly, the ice broke. Vanessa started to laugh and laugh. "Julio," she said, "I'll bet you are so clumsy that you fall down when you get out of bed in the morning. And now, here you are, making like you are going to be all over my lap with those napkins. Why don't you just sit down. Try to stay out of trouble for a couple of minutes."

Everyone, except Julio, laughed. "Vanessa, I'm really sorry," he said. "I was just trying to help out."

"I know," she said.

She reached across the table and took his hand. He started to pull his hand away. Vanessa withdrew her hand from his. Then she pulled back into her chair. She said quietly, "Hey, Julio. Let's try that again."

Julio responded by slowly reaching across the table for her hand. As their hands met, both he and Vanessa broke out into wide grins. Charmian squealed "Yes!" and threw her fist into the air. I slapped Julio on the back. At last, we were ready to start a normal conversation.

Suddenly, Julio was all relaxed. "So, tell me, Vanessa," he said, "How is your dancing going?"

"Just fine," she said, tugging on her hand. "I'll tell you what, Julio. If you will give me my hand back, I will tell you all about my dancing."

Julio was getting into it now. "Naw, that's OK. I'll just keep the hand. I didn't want to know anyway."

All of a sudden, she yanked her hand out of Julio's grip. "Thank you," she said.

"Now, let me tell you about my dancing. It is going very well. We have a troupe at school. Our teacher used to be with Alvin Ailey."

"Oh yeah, Alvin Ailey," said Julio. "Wasn't he a linebacker for the Giants?" All of a sudden, he sat up very straight. He had a slightly pained look on his face. "Hey," he said, "someone kicked me."

"That's right," Vanessa said. "If you are silly enough to look under the table, you will see my footprint on your trousers."

"I'm sorry," Julio said. "Sometimes, I open my mouth before I know what is coming out."

"Well, why don't you let me tell my story," Vanessa said. "If you start shooting off at the mouth, we'll just stuff it with these napkins." She picked up the ball of soggy napkins she used to clean up the spill.

"I'll help you," Charmian giggled. Julio just grinned. First, Vanessa told about her school dance company. They were going to give a performance at City College. Then she stopped for a moment. She became more serious.

"As you can tell," she said, "things are going really well for me. But I'm worried sick over my little brother, Hector. See, my mom is just beginning to get her life together again. She finally found another job. For a while, when she was out of work, she would become depressed. She drank a lot. Sometimes, she would hang out on the streets. She wouldn't come home for days. Hector had no real person to guide him. I tried to be that for him. But it's not working. Hector is a good kid. But he is running with the wrong crowd. I just know he is going to end up in serious trouble."

Julio was always touched by stories of family problems because he had so little family life of his own. "Vanessa," he said, "I'm really sorry to hear that. Do you think there is anything I can do?"

"Julio," said Vanessa with a big smile, "I thought you would never ask. You bet there is something you can do. He needs a big brother, a good influence, someone who will talk some sense into his head. Does this sound like a perfect job for you?"

"For me?" asked Julio. He hesitated. "Man, I don't know about that. Usually, I can keep myself out of trouble, but I have never thought about keeping other people out of trouble. That's a whole different ballgame."

Vanessa turned to Charmian and me. She said, "I'm going to take a chance with my hand again." Then she turned to Julio. She took his hand in hers and said, "If you can do it for yourself, you can do it for someone else." Julio looked down at her hand. Then he said, "I guess you are right."

"Well, it's nothing serious yet," she said. "You know he is only 14 years old. But he thinks he is all big and bad. He runs with this group of kids from his school who call themselves the B.W.A.—Boys with Attitude. They snatch chains and purses on the subway. They even shake down little kids for their lunch money. This is not exactly the kind of stuff you end up doing time for. But if this is what you're doing when you're

14, you will be doing something worse when you're 17. You'll be doing time before you get to your twenties.

"I am really afraid he is going to get hurt. There was this guy, Maurice, who had been down with the B.W.A. He had stolen this little kid's bicycle. The kid went howling home to his older brother. The older brother came out on the street with a baseball bat looking for Maurice.

"He walked up to Maurice with the bat behind his back. He said, 'How would you like to see a grand-slam home run?' Before Maurice knew what was happening, the guy pulled back the bat and caught Maurice across the jaw.

"His jaw was knocked right out of the socket. It had to be wired back into place. For a month after that, Maurice could not open his mouth. The only way he could eat was through a straw. Everything went into the blender. When he talked, he sounded like some kind of alien.

"Anyway, Hector showed up a couple of weeks ago with three chains. I asked him where they came from. He said some kid at school had given them to him. If he is out on the street snatching chains, it is just a matter of time before he gets seriously hurt."

Julio had been listening with great attention. I could see that he really was ready to get involved. I could also see that he had not let go of Vanessa's hand the whole time.

"Listen up, Julio," she said. "We are going to have to do something about this hand business. What's mine is mine. What's yours is yours. My hand is mine."

"We'll see about that," said Julio. Then he let go of her hand very slowly.

The Scar

Charmian and Vanessa left for their practice sessions. Charmian, who studied the flute, had an orchestra rehearsal. Vanessa had a dance class. This left Julio and me alone at the table. Julio looked very serious after they had gone.

He waited a moment. Then he said "picture that—me, a big brother to a young delinquent! I've never had a brother of my own. What if I let Vanessa down? Do you think I can really talk to her brother or do some good?"

I had known Julio for a long time. I had never seen him in quite this kind of situation. In fact, I wasn't entirely sure he would be able to pull it off. "Julio, my friend, there is only one way to find out.

Give it your best shot. I suggest that you and I go to Vanessa's neighborhood sometime this week after school. Let's see what this Hector kid is all about."

"Cool, man," said Julio, and that was how we left it.

He got back to Vanessa and said we would be down on Wednesday. She lived in the Washington Heights part of Manhattan, so it was an easy trip on the good old 1/9 train. We got off by the George Washington Bridge and went over to Broadway. We found Vanessa sitting on the stoop of her apartment house. After we both said "What's up?" Julio reached out his hand to shake hers.

She started to reach out her hand. Then she laughed and pulled it back. "Not just now, Julio. I may need this hand before the afternoon is over."

We sat on the steps for about ten minutes. Soon, the kids who were being let out of middle school started to show up. They all looked so small and harmless. I turned to Julio and said, "Man, remember when we were so small and so big and bad, all at the same time?"

Julio just laughed and said, "I don't remember. And if I did, I wouldn't want to admit it."

Most of the neighborhood kids had already passed. There was still no sign of Hector. I could see that Vanessa was starting to worry. Finally, we saw this skinny kid with his sneakers wide open and his pants hanging down around his butt. I could see that he had noticed us. He was not happy about it.

When he finally go up to the steps, Vanessa asked, "Hector, where have you been so long? You had me worried."

Before he even started to talk, I noticed that he had a fat lip. "Oh, I just had to stay a little later to talk with my teacher," said Hector.

"Talk with your teacher?" asked Vanessa. "I suppose your teacher gave you that fat lip? You know I can't stand it when you lie to me."

She motioned toward Julio and me. "I want you to meet two friends of mine. This is Vesey and Julio."

"Yeah, I know," he said in this unfriendly tone. "Julio is the one you like." Then he turned to Julio and said, "If you mess with my sister, my boys and I will come after you. You will wish you had never seen me. Have you got that straight?"

Julio turned to Vanessa and asked, "Is he always this charming, or is this just for me?"

I could see Vanessa was angry with Hector. "Julio is a good friend of mine. And—"

"Yeah, yeah," Hector interrupted. "Listen, keep your friends to yourself. I just want this guy here to know how he should treat my sister."

Julio had been looking Hector over the whole time. I could see he was getting a kick out of the whole business. "Man," he said. "You *are* bad. You know who you remind me of? You remind me of myself when I was 14 years old. Pants all down dragging on the ground. Shoes wide open. That's just how they wear clothes in jail. And then you have a lot of mouth for everyone. It's the only way to fly, my man.

"What about that fat lip you have? I bet you put the other guy in the hospital." Julio hesitated and saw that Hector was now not quite so sure of himself. "What?" Hector shouted. "The other guy is not in the hospital! Show me where he is and we'll beat him down. Just the three of us."

Hector was starting to have a hard time remaining all angry and bad. "The thing with the lip happened this way," he said. "This really big guy jumped me on the way home. He said I had ripped a chain off his sister in the subway. It wasn't even me. OK, so it was one of the B.W.A. crew. But I wasn't even with them the day they did that."

The story was coming apart faster than we had expected. "What is this snatching chains stuff?" asked Julio.

"Don't get the wrong idea," said Hector. "I don't get into that. But some of my guys do. They will take the subway down to 157th Street. Then they wait for kids coming home from school on the subway. There is no one in the station except for the guy selling tokens. So they can jump anyone they want to.

"I wasn't even there. But last week, the B.W.A.'s were waiting around. These girls came by. One of them had a chain with a head of Nefertiti on it. One of the guys grabbed the chain and ran.

"Anyway, someone in her group recognized us. The girl and her brother were waiting on the street when school was over. The other guys saw her out front. So they left by a side door. Since I didn't know anything about what happened, I walked right into it with her brother. He was really big. He swung on me before I could do anything. I did land a punch in his gut. Then he was gone."

Vanessa, Julio, and I just looked at each other. "Now how much of that are you guys going to believe?" Vanessa asked.

Julio just kept looking at Hector. Finally, he said, "That's really an amazing story. I just keep asking myself how this big brother knew to punch you if you hadn't even been there when the chain was snatched."

This one had him. After a while, Hector said, "I think he was just looking for someone to punch. I just happened to be there."

"Oh, OK," said Julio. "Now that makes sense. This big bruiser travels uptown 30 blocks to punch out middle-school kids he has never seen before. I have no problem with this. But now just one last question. How did you know this was the girl whose chain had been snatched if you hadn't even been there?"

Hector knew he was trapped. Turning to Vanessa, he said angrily, "What I do is my business. I sure don't need these two guys all in my business."

"You hold it right there, little man," shouted Vanessa. "Look at you! Fourteen years old and you are out on the street looking like a gangster. You have people from out of the neighborhood looking to beat you down. You are the only brother I've got. I don't intend to lose you to the streets."

"Hold it a minute, my man," said Julio. "Let me show you something." He then pulled up his shirt and showed Hector his famous scar. If you weren't ready for it, it could give you quite a scare. It ran from the base of the rib cage all the way down to where the appendix would be.

This time, he got Hector's attention. "Man, where did you get that?" he asked.

"Let me tell you something about this scar," said Julio. "I am lucky to be alive. I got this when I was 13. I was at least as bad as you are. This cut was almost the death of me. I wasn't even asking for trouble. Here's how it happened." We all sat back on the steps of Vanessa's stoop. When Julio got going on one of his stories, you would drop everything.

"Like I said," Julio went on, "I was only 13 when this happened. I had decided it was not safe to go home because my mom's boyfriend had moved in. He could be very rough with me. So I picked out this abandoned building over by White Plains Road where I would spend the night.

"I had a triple lunch in school that day. I knew I would not be eating again until lunch the next day. The one thing I always had on me when I was 13 or 14 was cigarettes. I don't smoke anymore. It's a nasty habit. But back then, I wouldn't go anywhere without stogs. I would smoke everywhere—on the bus, on the subway, in the school bathroom—anywhere it was not allowed.

"Anyway, I hung around on the street until it got dark. One by one, my friends went home. When I was all by myself, I went off to this abandoned building. I had only three cigarettes left to last me until the next day. I took out one to smoke before going to sleep.

"I lit it up. I could see the moon and the stars through the broken window frame. I felt real good. Just me and the spring sky in my own building. Then all of a sudden, I heard footsteps. Someone was coming toward me. At first, I could only see this shape. Then I saw it was a man. When I saw his face, I could see that he was crazy.

"At first, he just stared at me. Then he said 'cigarette.' That was all he said. Just 'cigarette.' I had only two left to last until I got back to school. I wasn't about to give one up. So I told him I was sorry. This was my last one. He stared at me for a moment in the dark. Then he suddenly lunged toward me. I felt a quick sting. He got up and then ran away. Suddenly, I could feel warm, wet blood all along my chest and stomach. I had been cut. Badly.

"I waited a while. I wanted to be sure this crazy man was gone. I stumbled to the street. Somehow, I made it to a corner just as a taxi was passing by. The driver got me to a hospital. The doctors gave me 227 stitches. If that taxi hadn't come along, I would have bled to death."

El Paradiso

I could see that Hector was looking a whole lot smaller now. He walked past us and up the steps. "I just wish everyone would stop sweating me, even if it is only for five minutes." Then he closed the door behind him.

Vanessa was looking really worried and unhappy. She turned to Julio and said, "Please don't tell Hector stories like that. If you have any more big scars, keep them to yourself. This boy has no one to look up to. You could make a difference in his life."

I could see that Julio was having a problem knowing how to take this. "What do you mean," he asked, "make a difference in his life? I mean I've got all I can do trying to make a difference in my own life. Here you are, talking about your kid brother."

Vanessa went on as though she had not even heard Julio speaking. Without thinking, she took Julio's hand in hers. "If you really want to make me happy, you will do something for that boy."

Julio had been listening closely, but I saw him sort of lose his train of thought when Vanessa took his hand. Vanessa noticed and said, "Julio, I don't think you are listening to me anymore. I am asking for your help." Then she started to try to pull her hand free.

He let her hand go. He became more serious. "Vanessa," he said, "Hector seems like a nice kid. I would really like to help you out. But I don't think there is a whole heck of a lot I can do. If you knew the kind of life I've had, you wouldn't be talking this way about my helping out your kid brother."

"You never know who you are going to help in life," Vanessa said. "Let me tell you something about myself. About three years ago, I ran with a very different crowd. I had never even thought about dancing. I was finishing middle school. I was developing real fast for my age. The girls I hung out with were part of a fast crowd. A lot of them had older boyfriends.

"There was this guy, Jaime, who had dropped out of school when he was 16. He was helping his father run his bodega. Jaime was about 20 years old at the time. He would always look at me with these real hungry eyes when he passed me on the street. He would look me over and tell me how 'fine' I was looking. He would always try to ask me out. I was just 14. But I looked older.

"Anyway, my mother knew Jaime was interested in me. All she said was that if I went out with him, I could stay with him. 'Don't come back to this house,' she warned.

"Even then I loved to dance. We would bring a radio out on the street. My friends and I would dance to the music—salsa, reggae, hip-hop, even rock. The guys would often stand around and watch.

Sometimes, they made smart remarks. Everyone said I was special when it came to dancing. I have to say it was something I loved to do.

"Anyway, Jaime knew about my interest in dancing. He also knew that I was dying to go to this club called El Paradiso. I knew I could never get in because I was underage. But I figured that if I went there with an older man, he could get me in. Then I would have a chance to see all the latest salsa dancing.

"One evening, Jaime came by while my friends and I were dancing on the street. I could feel his eyes watching my every move. All of a sudden, out of nowhere, he said I should come with him to the El Paradiso next Friday. Without even thinking, I said I would do it.

"When Friday came around, I made up a story about going to a friend's house. I even had her call up my mom. I went to my friend's house. Jaime picked me up there.

"As soon as we got to the club, I knew I had made a big mistake. Jaime had his hands all over me. When we danced, he tried to dance very close. I just wasn't ready for this kind of stuff from a guy.

"I kept trying to push him away. But he would keep coming onto me. Finally, I had a bright idea. I would dance the whole time, as fast and as far away from him as I could. I especially liked it when the music went fast because then I could do all my best steps. Jaime didn't have a chance to even try dancing close with me.

"Things went pretty well for about half an hour or so. I think I probably never danced better in my life. I noticed that quite a few people were watching me. At first, Jaime seemed to be pleased with all the attention. Then after a while, he became impatient. He wanted to sit down and get me to drink something. It was obvious that he was planning to have his way with me that evening. I knew there was going to be trouble before long.

"One tune had just finished, and the next one was about to start. Suddenly, Jaime started to pull at me. He wanted me to stop dancing. 'You need to sit down,' he kept saying. I said no. It looked as though he was going to get rough. I started to shout for him to leave me alone. People started to notice us.

"Suddenly, these two guys came up. They both were about 25 years old. Very quietly, they told Jaime that he should let me loose. He knew he wasn't going to be able to beat them both down. He backed off. As he walked away, he cursed at me. The two men asked if I would like to sit with them. I said yes.

"Anyway, this turned out to be my lucky night. The first thing one of the men said when I had calmed down was that I was one beautiful dancer. He suggested that I come audition for a production they would be doing in a couple of months.

"I couldn't believe how lucky I had been. Here I had disobeyed my mother and told her a lie. Then I went to a bar with an older man. Now I was getting the break of my life.

"The next weekend I went in for the audition. I made it as a member of the chorus. The dance teacher, a really nice guy named Oliver, kept telling me how much talent I had. He also told me about the arts program in the city high schools. It's because of him that I have gotten to where I am today.

"The point of all this is that the right person at the right time can make all the difference in another person's life. I would just love to see you become that person for Hector."

I could see that the story had made a real impression on Julio. He was staring at Vanessa, deep in thought. Finally, he turned to her and said, "Vanessa, maybe you are right. Maybe I could make a difference in the life of another person. I would sure like to give it a try."

I could see Vanessa looking all happy. Julio still looked unsure. He went on, "But what am I going to do? How do you picture this happening?"

This seemed like a good question to me. I was glad not to be in Julio's position just now. But Vanessa had no problem. "It is easy, Julio," she said. "All you have to do is to be there and be yourself. What Hector needs is a person he respects. He needs someone who will care about him.

"Never mind the big promises and the big words," said Vanessa. "When does he get into trouble? The answer to that one is, right after school. Suppose he were to just happen to run into you after school and never hook up with his friends? It could be the most natural thing in the world. Like I was saying, it is not a matter of big ideas. It is just a matter of being there."

"Actually," said Julio, "this could work out. He comes out of school an hour later than I do. I could be at his school when he gets out." I could see this twinkle come into Julio's eye. He reached out and took Vanessa's hand. "Yes," he said, "I can see it. I'll just show up. And let me say one more thing." He was really getting into it now. "The fact that I have this big scar is going to help. I can tell you that got his attention."

Vanessa looked down at her hand and said, "Well, I see you are already taking care of business." Then she reached with her other hand and stroked his cheek. He got all red in the face. Vanessa continued speaking. "Hector is out of school at four o'clock tomorrow afternoon. I am dying to hear how things go."

4 Boys with Attitude

Julio and I took the subway back uptown. I could see that he was both happy and worried. "Well," he said, "I think she likes me. But this stuff with Hector—I don't know about that." He paused for a moment and then went on. "But for this woman, I am willing to try anything."

"I am sure you can do it," I said. "Behind all that noise and attitude, Hector seems like he may not be so bad."

"I am sure I can do it," said Julio, "and you are going to be coming with me."

"Now wait a minute," I said. "This is your woman and your woman's wild kid brother. Where do I come into all this?"

"I don't want to get into it with this crew all by myself. I just know that things will go better if I have some backup."

I knew he was right. Besides, I really had nothing better to do. We agreed that we would be on the street the next day when school let out. We wanted to see just what was up with the B.W.A.

The next day we got out of school at three o'clock. We took the subway right down to the Washington Heights area. We were in front of the school at about a quarter of four. At four, the school bell rang. You could hear cheers, running, and shouting. In a couple of minutes kids started to come out of the building. First, we saw the little ones shouting and laughing. Then we saw the older ones in groups of three or four.

After about five minutes, Hector came out with four other guys. The first thing they did when they came out was to pull out their belts and take the laces out of their sneakers. They pulled their pants down so you could see the tops of their boxers. Then they all looked at one another and laughed. One of them said, "Let's hear it for the B.W.A.!"

"I think this is my moment," said Julio. He walked up to Hector. "Yo, Hector, whazzup?" You remember me yesterday— 227 stitches?"

At first, Hector hesitated. I could see he was not sure how his boys would feel about a couple of strangers. Then I could see he was coming around. "Yo, guys," he said to the others, "look at the scar this man has. Julio, show them your scar."

Julio came over to the group and lifted his shirt. Everyone looked at him wide-eyed. One of them asked, "Say, man, where did you get that?"

"I got it by being where I wasn't supposed to be," said Julio.

I could see that this was not the answer they wanted to hear. Julio went on. "This cut almost cost me my life. I used to do all kinds of wild and stupid stuff. But after this, I decided I was lucky to be alive. It was time to straighten out my life."

One of the guys whom they called Big Junior looked sort of sour. He said, "Man, this is whack. Let's get out of here. Who wants to hear about this guy's stupid scar?"

"Yeah, yeah," said Julio, "I know all about you guys. You are all big and bad. Nobody can touch you. It's you crazy young guys who get hurt all the time. You pull some stupid stuff, and a father or older brother comes after you. Then you'll be getting fitted with a new set of teeth."

Big Junior wasn't going to let this pass. "Get out of here, man. The stuff we do—no one is going to give us any grief."

Julio saw that his chance was coming. "Oh yeah?" he asked. "Why don't you tell me about it? Let me decide how dangerous it is."

"All's we do is ride around on the subway. Sometimes, we mess with people if we feel like it," said Big Junior.

"What do you mean—you *mess with people*?" asked Julio.

Another kid—he called himself Little J, although he must have been six feet and

210 pounds of baby fat—wanted to get into the conversation. "Like last week," said Little J, "we were messing with these kids at the Dyckman Street Station. They're real punks. They travel only one or two together. But there are always five or six of us. We just stopped them on the steps and roughed them down. They are such herbs that they give up their wallets, their subway passes, and their bookbags. No problem."

Now Big Junior wanted to get into the conversation. "Then there are these girls with chains and necklaces. We just ask them real nice to give up their stuff. And, they just do it. They're dumb kids."

I could tell that this kind of stuff was not going to be safe day after day. I could see that Julio was getting the same idea. "I have to say," Julio said, "that sounds very easy. But what happens when there are more of them than you? What if an older brother comes around? Has that ever happened?"

There was silence for a few minutes. Finally Hector spoke up. "Yes, sometimes there is trouble." Then he turned to the other B.W.A.'s and said, "Remember, right before we got into middle school, this guy Floyd got killed?"

They were all quiet. Then Hector went on. "Floyd and these four other kids were doing the same kind of stuff we do. You know, hanging out and snatching stuff from smaller kids. Anyway, he and his posse were at the 149th Street station doing this. They had snatched a whole lot of change and subway passes. They had even taken the sneakers right off a couple of kids right there in the subway station.

"They were having a good time of it. They thought they would never get caught. It turned out they had hit the same kid twice. They took his Walkman and a week later they took his sneakers. This kid had an older brother. The older brother had his posse. Anyway, Floyd and his crew were there in the 149th Street station for more than two weeks. That's already a mistake, because people will come looking for you.

"On this particular day, Floyd was there with his crew. All of a sudden about eight big kids showed up with baseball bats, along with the guy who had lost his Walkman and his sneakers. He pointed to Floyd and his crew. With that, the big kids just came down the steps swinging. They caught one kid in Floyd's crew. Knocked him out. Cold. Floyd knew he was going to get his. He was really scared. He decided to run across the tracks. The baseball bats were so close behind him that he did not take a whole lot of time to see if things were safe. He just jumped off the platform and started toward the other side. There was a train coming. He was able to jump out of the way. But he had to jump so fast that he came down on the third rail of the tracks on the other side.

"Everyone said there was this crack like a thunderstorm. There was a flash of lightning and a nasty smell of burned flesh. Floyd was dead in a second. That was the end of the whole posse. The rest of them just went home or to the basketball hoops after school from then on. No more chain snatching. No more subway terror."

This was quite a story. All of us were quiet after hearing it. Hector had really talked himself out.

Julio figured this had to be his moment to make a pitch. "So, doesn't this tell you something?" he asked. "If you mess with people, they will come and find you. If you are a bunch of little 14-year-old kids, someone is going to get hurt. Doesn't that make sense?"

They weren't ready for this yet. Big Junior was the first one to speak. "Naw, man, that was then and this is now. We never stay around the same station for more than a day or two. Then we go to another part of the city. Sometimes, we go up to the Bronx. Or we will go down to 96th Street and take the train uptown.

"The trick is to keep moving. You shake down different kids at different times. Shoot, I have never seen the same kid twice. We're too fast." Then Big Junior slapped hands with Little J. They both laughed.

Julio knew he just wasn't making it. At least not this time. "OK, guys," he said. "Don't say I didn't warn you, and don't come running to me when trouble comes down."

The B.W.A.'s started to walk away. I could see that Hector was hanging back. Julio figured he might have one more chance. "Yo, Hector, man, you don't need to go do that stupid stuff."

We could see that Hector was being pulled in both directions. Julio said, "Remember that big scar I showed you? And remember the story of that guy Floyd, who got fried on the third rail? Someday, that's going to be you. Maybe not today, maybe not this year, maybe not until your twenties. But believe me, you play that street game, and the only thing you can be sure of is that you will pay with your life."

I had never heard Julio speak so well and so clearly. I gave him a pat on the back.

I think that Hector was convinced. He was just not ready to break away from his friends yet.

The rest of the crew was already down at the corner. Big Junior turned and shouted, "Let's move out, Hector. You don't want to hang out with those guys. They're too old for you."

I could hear the other members of the B.W.A. laugh when Big Junior said this.

Hector grabbed Julio's hand. He shook it and said, "Thanks man. I know you want what's right for me. But, believe me, I know what I am doing. I know how to stay out of the way of trouble. Maybe next time. But this time, I am going to run with my crew." With that he was off at a full run. His open sneakers clomped on the ground and his shorts rode over the top of his pants.

5 Hector's Luck Runs Out

Julio looked at me and said, "I don't have a good feeling about this. Hector is just the kind of fool who gets badly hurt before he even knows what has hit him."

We took the subway back uptown to the Bronx. I could see that Julio was not happy with the way things had gone. We would have a chance that night to tell the whole story to Vanessa. It was Thursday, the day Charmian and I always have our "study date." We had been doing this for two months. As long as we kept our grades up, everything was fine. Tonight, we were including Julio and Vanessa. We decided to meet at Vanessa's place.

When we all got there at 7:15, I knew something was wrong. Vanessa's mother was very quiet as she let us in. She looked worried.

Vanessa also looked worried. She whispered to us in a nervous voice, "Hector didn't come home for dinner." This was something that just never happened unless there was an emergency. We all tried to reassure Vanessa that everything was fine. Actually, we weren't all that sure that everything was fine.

First, Julio told Vanessa about his conversation with Hector. He added that Hector had almost decided to stay back. Vanessa was obviously touched that Julio had tried so hard. She told him not to feel bad that Hector had gone out anyway. "After all," she said, "what can happen to him?"

We all gathered around the dining table. We took out our books. But we just sat there looking at each other and at the clock. Finally, the phone rang. Vanessa jumped up. "I'll get it mom," she shouted. It was Big Junior's mother asking if we had any idea where he might be. He had also missed dinner. Now we knew something was wrong.

We spent another half hour looking at each other and at the clock. The phone rang. It was Big Junior's mother again. She said her boy was in the hospital. She did not know about the other five. A policeman had just called to say that there had been some kind of a fight. Big Junior had a broken arm.

Vanessa's mom was very upset. She looked at Vanessa. "Maybe we should go to the police station," she said.

At that moment, the phone started to ring. Vanessa jumped up and grabbed it. At first she was excited. Then she was confused. She turned around and said, "Julio, it's for you."

Julio picked up the phone. "Hello," he said, "Who is this?" Then his face became all lively and excited. "Hector! Man, what happened? Where in the world are you? Are you all right?"

Then Julio was quiet. Every now and then, Julio would say, "Yeah," or "That's tough, man," or "I know what you're talking about." This went on for about ten minutes. Julio finally said, "OK, Hector, we're out of here. We'll see you in about half an hour."

We couldn't wait to hear what had happened. We all turned on Julio at once with questions. It seems that Hector and the B.W.A.'s had been taken in by the police. Hector was down at the precinct waiting for a responsible family member to pick him up.

Julio, Vanessa's mom, and I took a taxi to the precinct. Vanessa and Charmian stayed back in case there were any more phone calls.

When they brought Hector up to the desk, he didn't look all that big and bad anymore. He sort of hung his head as we took him out.

Because there were so many of us, we decided to take a cab back. When we got home, we all sat down at the table and stared at Hector. "OK," said Vanessa, "Let's hear it all. The whole story. But before you even start, I want to know why you didn't even ask to speak with me or mom when you phoned. What was the idea of asking for Julio?"

Hector took a deep breath. "OK. First, I asked for Julio because I felt he really believes in me. You and mom always give me a hard time. See, I think behind it all, you two think I am really a gangster. Anyway, I don't want to hear about gangsters for a long time."

"Well that's good news," said Vanessa. "Now tell us what kind of stupid stuff you were doing that got you into jail and got your friend into the hospital with a broken arm."

I could see that he wasn't going to enjoy this. But he had no place to hide. "Well," Hector said, "You know how the B.W.A. likes to hang out and bother kids. The problem with that kind of stuff is that if you bother the same kids too many times, they will come after you with their brothers and fathers. So you need to remember where you've been and how long ago.

"We had been around this neighborhood to the east of Jerome Avenue, but no one could remember whether it had been two weeks or two months ago. Yesterday was the first of the month, which means that all the school kids have new subway and bus passes. We like taking the kids' bus passes.

"Anyway, we went to this neighborhood where all these fifth and sixth graders were hanging out. It was around 4:30 in the afternoon. We thought we could shake them down for a few things.

"There were six of us. Usually, we just come down the street looking hard and mean. Some kids see us coming and cross to the other side. Others don't notice until we are right on top of them.

"When that happens, three of us grab up one kid. Then we tell him to give us everything in his pockets. This went fine the first time. We got a couple of bucks in change and a Snoop Doggy Dog tape. There were a couple of kids with the kid we grabbed. We saw them run away. But, we didn't really think about it at that time.

We realize now that they had gone off to get reinforcements.

"We went up another couple of blocks and then turned off to the left. Again there was this group of about five little kids. We shook down two of them. Then we turned around and went back up toward Jerome Avenue.

"This was our big mistake. When you do this kind of stuff, you never want to go back on your tracks. Always keep moving ahead. Then, if there are people out looking for you, they'll have trouble finding you.

"Anyway, we got up to Jerome Avenue. Out of the corner of my eye, I noticed this group of eight kids. They must have been 16 or 17 years old. For some reason, I just didn't think that this might mean trouble for us. We just went on to another cross street. We started to cruise around for some new victims. As we came around the corner at the end of this street, there were four of the kids we had been messing with earlier. They were with these eight older kids.

"The younger kids pointed to us and said, 'These are the ones.' We all started to run off in different directions. These two kids, who were just bigger and faster, caught every one of us. They brought us back to the corner.

"One of them had a baseball bat. He said he would like to bang out our brains right there. But first he wanted to hear what we had to say for ourselves. We were all looking down at the ground, feeling real foolish and real scared.

"Then one of the little kids pointed to Big Junior. The kid said Big Junior was the one who had punched him in the gut and taken his Walkman. The guy with the bat walked over to Big Junior. He told him to empty his pockets.

"Big Junior moved real slow. He knew the Walkman was going to come up. The guy with the bat kept telling him to hurry up. Big Junior kept stalling. Finally, he got to his last pocket. Out came the Walkman. I could see that the guy with the bat was really angry.

"He didn't say anything. He just raised the bat and came down hard and fast. Big Junior put out his arm to catch the blow. You could hear the arm bone snap like a twig. It must have really hurt. Big Junior just went down on his knees and started to make this whining noise. It was almost like the noise you hear from a hurt dog.

"After Big Junior, I could see they were getting ready to work over the rest of us. Just then, a patrol car came around the corner. I have never been happier to see the police. They could see the bat and Big Junior down on his knees. They came over and asked what had happened.

"One of the older kids told the entire story about how we had jumped the little kids and taken their stuff. Normally, we would have denied everything. But there was Big Junior with this kid's Walkman.

"The police gave us a real talking to. First, they said they were taking us down to the station. Then they lectured us. They said that hoodlums like us kept decent people from feeling safe on the street—even at 4:00 in the afternoon.

"The police also took in the guy who used the bat on Big Junior. They put us all in a cell together. I was glad that they didn't let that guy bring his bat into the cell."

6 Three's a Crowd

There was no need to lecture Hector. We could see that he had been scared by the entire adventure.

By now it was close to midnight. We did not get much studying done on our study date. We all went home. I didn't see Julio again until the weekend. I was walking along Broadway and 215th Street. Suddenly, I heard someone shout my name. It was Julio. He was all excited. He said he had a whole lot to tell me. I said we should go have a slice of pizza together. Julio said he couldn't do that. He had to save his money. I told him I didn't know he even had any money to save. I said "Hey man, the pizza will be on me."

When we sat down in the pizza parlor, I asked him what was going on. He said, "I want to get Vanessa a ring. I want her to have something from me that is with her all the time. I have taken a job as a messenger downtown. I borrowed a bicycle. I can make $50 in a four-hour day. I already have $175."

This was a new side of Julio for me. I won't say that he was lazy. But the picture of him burning up the streets on a bicycle to deliver messages in midtown took some getting used to. "So tell me more. What made you decide that Vanessa has to have a ring from you?"

"After all that stuff with Hector, she has been so nice to me. She told me that no one has ever done more for Hector than I have. She says she likes me. I have never had a relationship like this with a girl. It's about being close and really appreciating each other. I know you understand," he said.

"Of course," I said. "Things are like that between Charmian and me. Man, I'm really happy for you," I continued.

He rushed through his pizza. He had a job in an hour. He was going to clean and polish a couple of cars in the neighborhood at $30 each. As he left, he said he had a date with Vanessa that night. He promised to fill me in the next day. I told him I would be at our favorite diner at 11:30.

When he showed up the next day, he didn't look quite as happy as he had been the day before. I asked, "So what's up with the date, Julio? How did things go between you and Vanessa last night?"

"Between me and Vanessa?" he snapped. "You mean between me, Vanessa, and Hector. Can you believe this? The three of us went to the movies together!"

I could see that he was angry, but I couldn't help laughing. "I want to hear this. How did you end up taking Hector to the movies?"

"Well," he said, "we had it all planned. We were going to go to an early show and then have dinner together. We planned to come back to her place. Everyone was going to be out. It was a perfect plan.

"But I knew the plan wasn't going to be all that perfect when I arrived to pick her up for the movies. She let me in the door. There was Hector sitting on the floor eating popcorn and watching a movie on television. Now don't get me wrong. I really like Hector. I feel like he is sort of a younger brother to me now. So I am not going to be hard on him or anything.

"Anyway, there he is watching the TV and eating popcorn. I ask him what's up. Then I tell him I'll see him later. Vanessa and I start to head for the door. He says to wait a minute and asks where we are going. I tell him we are in a hurry because we have to catch the 4:00 movie. He says 'Great. I've been waiting for the longest time to see that show. I'm coming with you.'

"Before I can say anything, he has grabbed his hat and turned off the television set. He quickly writes a note for his mother who's visiting a girlfriend. Then he leaps out the door in front of us and onto the steps. I look over toward

Vanessa like she should say something to him.

"She does manage to say, 'Hector, this is supposed to be a date for me with Julio.' Hector suddenly looked so sad—I actually thought he was going to cry. So I told him it would be OK for him to come along with us to the movies.

"We get to the movies. We each get a soda and I buy a big tub of popcorn for us to share. Every time I try to put my arm around Vanessa or hold her hand, Hector says, 'Yo, Julio, could you pass me over some popcorn?'

"Finally I give him the whole tub. I put my arm around Vanessa. Two seconds later, Hector gets up. Now he says he has to go to the bathroom. While he was gone, Vanessa and I were kissing like crazy. We knew he would be right back.

"Next thing I know, I'm kissing Vanessa and there is Hector stepping all over my feet to get back to his seat.

"Pretty soon he had been to the bathroom twice. He dropped his keys. He went out to buy a second soda. And he actually phoned one of his buddies.

"By now I just had to give up. When I wasn't angry at Hector, I had to laugh. Vanessa laughed also. She finally leaned over and whispered to me, 'Don't worry. I'll make it up to you later on.'

"Well, there was no later on. Vanessa and I went out to dinner. I don't have to tell you who was there with us. Then came the part I had really been looking forward to—back to the apartment—just the two of us. Well, it was just the three of us. I kept asking Hector if he didn't have a friend he wanted to call or a television show he was dying to see.

"He just kept acting stupid. He said he didn't want to leave us alone because we might get bored. Can you believe this boy? I would have been more upset if Vanessa had not been so happy about the whole thing. Every time Hector left the room, she would tell me that I was the first older person he had ever listened to. She kept saying 'Julio, I just don't know how to thank you enough.'

"Then she would get this little twinkle in her eye and say, 'Actually, I know exactly how to thank you.' When she talks that way, she makes me really crazy. So, hey, I figure I can put up with Hector's stuff for a little longer. Anyway, I am going to be seeing her again tonight. This time, I have a plan."

With that he left. Julio seemed to be happier now. Obviously, both Vanessa and Hector were good for him, although he may not have seen it exactly that way.

I didn't see him for another week. But when I did see him, he was all smiles. I knew that he had taken care of the Hector problem. I was eager to hear what he had done. I took him out for pizza again. I told him I would pick up the tab if he would tell me all.

First he said, "Wait a minute. Let me show you the ring I got her." He pulled out a small ring with this sort of white-pink-blue stone that seemed to shine from within. I am not really into this stuff. But I had to admit that it was beautiful. He said it was an opal. It had cost him $350. He was going to give it to her that night. "I am not going to ask her to marry me. Someday, however, that is what I would like to do. For now, I am going to ask her to go with me for the rest of her life. Not marry, just go with me. I think she will go for it."

"Now I want to hear about your date last weekend," I said. "You know, you and Vanessa and Hector."

He laughed, "That's how it started. But that is not how it ended."

"So what did you do?" I asked.

"It was just like the last time," he said. "We went to the movies. Hector went with us. He was all over the place. Then we started playing the same game back on him. I spilled my drink on his shoes. Vanessa got up to go to the powder room during one of the really exciting parts. She stood right in front of Hector until the action was over.

"When the popcorn was done, I sent him out to buy some more with his own money. Then Vanessa and I kept pestering him to give us some. He kept saying we should keep it. We refused. We just kept giving it back to him. Finally, I accidentally dumped the entire container in his lap.

"He was beginning to get what was going on. But he still didn't want to admit it. As the movie became more exciting, I kept leaning over and asking him how he liked it. People around us were telling us to shut up. Hector was getting really embarrassed.

"Finally he said, 'If you don't stop acting stupid, I'm leaving.' Vanessa and I just leaned over and looked at him. Both of us were smiling. At first he looked hurt. Then he smiled. He said, 'I think I get it. I'm out of here. I'll see you guys later.'

"We left the movie early. We went out for dinner. Then we went to Vanessa's house. At a quarter of eight we could see Hector outside. He was walking up and down the street. At exactly 8:00, he had his key in the door. He jumped into the apartment.

"We had it perfectly staged. I was in one corner of the room reading the encyclopedia. Vanessa was sitting in the other corner knitting. We just grinned at Hector. At first he looked sort of silly. Then he burst out laughing."